WORTH THE PAIN

EASTER DEVOTIONAL

PASTOR BOB COY

Compiled by Margaret DeStefano
Edited by Ana Steele, Ph.D.
Cover and Interior Design by Deven Christopher
Project Management by The Caleb Group

Printed in the United States of America

CONTENTS

INTRODUCTION
That Day In Between

Have you ever stopped to wonder about that day in between? That day that was no more than a blip on the screen of eternity and took place between the crucifixion and the resurrection? We get so caught up in the sorrow of Christ's suffering and the exuberance of His resurrection that we don't often stop to consider what was going on in between these two contrasting occurrences.

We know from the recorded stories of the Gospels that that day fell within the week of Unleavened Bread, more popularly known today as Passover. Passover started with the cleansing of every Jewish home of any trace of leaven. It was a time of remembrance and a time of contemplation of God's saving character. God's instructions to His people for preparing and observing the Passover feast throughout time are given in detail in Exodus Chapter 12:

"Speak to all the congregation of Israel, saying: 'On the tenth *day* of this month every man shall take for himself a lamb, according to the house of *his* father, a lamb for a household...Your lamb shall be without blemish, a male of the first year...Then the whole assembly of the congregation of Israel shall kill it at twilight. And they shall take *some* of the blood and put *it* on the two doorposts and on the lintel of the houses where they eat it...It is *the* Lord's Passover. For I will pass through the land of Egypt on that night, and will strike all the firstborn in the land of Egypt, both man and beast; and against all the gods of Egypt I will execute judgment: I *am* the LORD. Now the blood shall be a sign for you on the houses where you *are*. And when I see the blood, I will pass over you; and the plague shall not be on you to destroy *you* when I strike the land of Egypt. So this day shall be to you a memorial...You shall keep it as a feast by an everlasting ordinance.'" (Exodus 12:3, 5-7, 11-14 NKJV)

For every year since the first Passover, even in the year that Jesus was crucified, the Israelites observed this feast day in remembrance of what God had done for them in Egypt. For the religious rulers who had been instrumental in Christ's crucifixion, one has to wonder why the drama that had just played out so powerfully before their very eyes did not even spark a correlation in their minds as they rested on that Sabbath day in between and contemplated the first Passover. Or as they thought back to the Father of their Faith, Abraham, and his great and prophetic statement of faith to Isaac:

"...My son, God will provide himself a lamb for a burnt offering..." (Genesis 22:8 KJV)

Did the compelling words that John the Baptist had cried out to them at the Jordan River come to their minds at all?

"I am not the Christ...but there stands One among you whom you do not know. It is He who, coming after me, is preferred before me, whose sandal strap I am not worthy to loose." ...The next day John saw Jesus coming toward him, and said, "Behold! The Lamb of God who takes away the sin of the world!" (John 1:20, 26-27, 29 NKJV)

When the religious leaders asked the soldiers to break the legs of the men being crucified to get them off the cross before the High Holy Day, did these leaders not find it odd that the soldiers did not have to break Jesus' legs? Did they not remember God's words in Exodus?

"In one house it shall be eaten; you shall not carry any of the flesh outside the house, nor shall you break one of its bones." (Exodus 12:46 NKJV)

But when they came to Jesus and saw that He was already dead, they did not break His legs. (John 19:33 NKJV)

Did it ever dawn on these men on that Sabbath day of contemplation that there was a divine reason that crucifixions were forbidden within the gates of the city?

"You may not sacrifice the Passover within any of your gates which the LORD your God gives you." (Deuteronomy 16:5 NKJV)

Therefore Jesus also, that He might sanctify the people with His own blood, suffered outside the gate. (Hebrews 13:12 NKJV)

On that day in between, when they remembered their forefathers' deliverance in Egypt and considered their present oppression by the Roman government, do you think it triggered any thoughts of the promised Messiah? As they considered the Messianic prophecies written hundreds of years before Jesus ever walked the earth, why did they not connect the many similarities to Jesus' crucifixion?

But He *was* wounded for our transgressions, He *was* bruised for our iniquities; The chastisement for our peace *was* upon Him, And by His stripes we are healed. (Isaiah 53:5 NKJV)

So then Pilate took Jesus and scourged *Him*. (John 19:1 NKJV)

He was oppressed and He was afflicted, Yet He opened not His mouth; He was led as a lamb to the slaughter, And as a sheep before its shearers is silent, So He opened not His mouth. (Isaiah 53:7 NKJV)

Then Pilate said to Him, "Do You not hear how many things they testify against You?" But He answered him not one word, so that the governor marveled greatly. (Matthew 27:13-14 NKJV)

All who see me mock me; they hurl insults, shaking their heads: "He trusts in the LORD; let the LORD rescue him. Let him deliver him, since he delights in him." (Psalms 22:7-8 NIV)

Those who passed by hurled insults at him, shaking their heads and saying, "...save yourself! Come down from the cross, if you are the Son of God!" In the same way the chief priests, the teachers of the law and the elders mocked him... "He trusts in God. Let God rescue him now if he wants him." (Matthew 27:39-43 NIV)

My God, My God, why have You forsaken Me? Why are You so far from helping Me, And from the words of My groaning? (Psalms 22:1 NKJV)

And about the ninth hour Jesus cried out with a loud voice, saying, "Eli, Eli, lama sabachthani?" that is, "My God, My God, why have You forsaken Me?" (Matthew 27:46 NKJV)

They divide My garments among them, And for My clothing they cast lots. (Psalms 22:18 NKJV)

Then the soldiers, when they had crucified Jesus, took His garments and made four parts, to each soldier a part, and also the tunic. Now the tunic was without seam, woven from the top in one piece. They said therefore among themselves, "Let us not tear it, but cast lots for it, whose it shall be," that the Scripture might be fulfilled which says: "They divided My garments among them, And for My clothing they cast lots." Therefore the soldiers did these things. (John 19:23-24 NKJV)

Easter, like Passover, is a time to be silent and remember. The empty tomb reminds us that God has not left us or forsaken us. Jesus Himself promised:

"In My Father's house are many mansions; if *it were* not *so*, I would have told you. I go to prepare a place for you. And if I go and prepare a place for you, I will come again and receive you to Myself; that where I am, *there* you may be also." (John 14:2-3 NKJV)

This Easter, remember that Jesus is coming back. When He left the empty tomb, He showed the world that His mission here was accomplished. He paid the price for your sins and went to prepare a heavenly home for those who dare to believe the unbelievable goodness of God, who sent His Son to die for us.

From His death by crucifixion to the resurrection life, Jesus offers you a midpoint of rest – a Sabbath. No one can go from death to life everlasting without stopping in between to rest in the finished work of the cross. When you do, the blood of Christ becomes the lamb's blood on the doorpost of your heart that signals death to pass over.

For if the blood of bulls and goats and the ashes of a heifer, sprinkling the unclean, sanctifies for the purifying of the flesh, how much more shall the blood of Christ, who through the eternal Spirit offered Himself without spot to God, cleanse your conscience from dead works to serve the living God? (Hebrews 9:13-14 NKJV)

For by grace you have been saved through faith, and that not of yourselves; *it is* the gift of God, not of works, lest anyone should boast. (Ephesians 2:8-9 NKJV)

For He made Him who knew no sin *to be* sin for us, that we might become the righteousness of God in Him. (2 Corinthians 5:21 NKJV)

Therefore purge out the old leaven, that you may be a new lump, since you truly are unleavened. For indeed Christ, our Passover, was sacrificed for us. (1 Corinthians 5:7 NKJV)

THE SUPREMACY OF HUMILITY

"For I have given you an example, that you should do as I have done to you. Most assuredly, I say to you, a servant is not greater than his master; nor is he who is sent greater than he who sent him. If you know these things, blessed are you if you do them." (John 13:15-17 NKJV)

Jesus' gesture in the upper room jarred the disciples. In an attitude of unbelief and astonishment, they watched their Master take on the garments of a servant and stoop down to wash their feet. What was racing through their minds as they sat there mesmerized by this Man of Miracles and His endless ability to stun them into the reality of His world? Could they have been thinking about the time He raised Lazarus from the dead, or the time He healed the ten lepers, or the time He turned over the tables in the temple? Or perhaps they pictured Him walking on the water in the midst of the storm that had them fighting for their lives? No matter what memory of Jesus they conjured up, it did not fit the form of the One who was now stooping humbly before them, gently washing the dirt and dust from their foul feet. The moment was so intense and the picture so poignant that Peter burst forth with that which was probably foremost on each of their hearts:

"...You shall never wash my feet!" (John 13:8 NKJV)

Each disciple knew that he should be the one washing the feet of Jesus. They had spent the last three years watching this Man perform miracles, teach with the authority of God, and make mincemeat out of the Pharisees. They had come to expect that whatever happened, Jesus could handle it, but at that moment they were having a very difficult time handling this unexpected act of outright humility. They knew Jesus was gentle because they had seen Him with the parents whose daughter He raised from the dead. They knew He was kind because they had watched Him with the woman caught in adultery. His compassion was unquestionable as they looked on while He fed the thousands that followed Him with five loaves and two fishes. But they had missed the underlying humility in everything Jesus had done, perhaps because it had always been masked in an overtone of miraculous power. Their arguments over who would be the greatest made it obvious that they had focused on His might rather than His Spirit. They wanted everything to do with the majesty side of the ministry, but this Servant's heart and attitude was a real problem for them. As if Jesus had read their minds, He made it quite clear that the package is inseparable. You cannot have one without the other.

Jesus answered him, "If I do not wash you, you have no part with Me." (John 13:8b NKJV)

Jesus had given the disciples an example, and lest they misunderstand and think the example was literally the foot washing itself, He explained further that the standard He had set was one of humility. The act of washing feet in Jesus' day was the most lowly, insignificant task imaginable and reserved for the least (in status) of the household. Assuming this role, Jesus set the pattern, the protocol, and the precedent for all who would choose to follow Him. If He was willing to humble Himself to the point of washing feet, then His disciples must also be willing to be as humble.

It is only when we cross the barrier of pride that we discover the most remarkable miracles of all – the joy, peace, and strength found in humility. This is why many of us cannot find true fulfillment. We are looking for it in the wrong place – at the top. Christ clearly sets the example and shows us that it is found at the bottom. When we give away our rights to be first, we enter that place where true contentment is found because it is in this place that God dwells:

For thus says the High and Lofty One Who inhabits eternity, whose name is Holy: "I dwell in the high and holy place, With him who has a contrite and humble spirit, To revive the spirit of the humble, And to revive the heart of the contrite ones..." (Isaiah 57:15 NKJV)

If we consider Christ our Master, then we must follow the model of His humility. In His humble example of being last, we will find the fulfillment that our soul seeks. This is another powerful principle in the paradox of God's promises.

"For whoever desires to save his life will lose it, but whoever loses his life for My sake will find it." (Matthew 16:25 NKJV)

A CLOSER LOOK

Describe a time when you experienced the power of humility in your own life.

What reaction do you have when someone cuts in front of you at the grocery store, in the bank line, or on the highway? How could humility help you overcome your feelings of frustration?

Write a brief paragraph about what happens in your heart when you consider the humility of God in comparison to His majesty.

What areas of your life would you have to lose in order to find the humble life of Christ?

PALMS PIERCED WITH NAILS

Then some began to spit on Him, and to blindfold Him, and to beat Him, and to say to Him, "Prophesy!" And the officers struck Him with the palms of their hands. (Mark 14:65 NKJV)

The scene had to be surreal in heaven as the angels watched in horror the creation desecrating the Creator. With mouths made for praise came mockery and defilement. In their own blindness, these men tried to blind Omniscience. How absurd! How incredulous! The angels must have stood in amazement as they witnessed a love so great that it would suffer the humiliation and attacks from its object of affection just to restore the relationship lost in the Garden of Eden.

With every insult and with each blow, the humanity of Christ was put to the test. At any instant, He could have exercised His majesty. He could have told them not only their names, but how many hairs each had on his head. He could have turned their spit to lead and sealed their mouths permanently. He could have burned through the blindfold with His blazing eyes of fire. He could have called a legion of angels to fight on His behalf.

It is not recorded how long this display of masochistic cruelty lasted, but when one considers that the entire ordeal from His arrest to His crucifixion and death was probably 18 hours, that would be 64,800 seconds. That would be 64,800 times Christ said 'no' to the temptation to put an end to God's will in His life. That would be 64,800 times He chose us over Himself. That would be 64,800 times He accessed the power of the Holy Spirit within Him to lay down this life and accomplish the Father's will.

Although they spat on Him, blindfolded Him, mocked Him, and beat Him, He never gave up the goal set before Him: to die for their sins so that the Scriptures concerning the nail-pierced palms of His hands would be fulfilled. Those scars will remain for eternity as an everlasting symbol of God's unfailing love for us:

But Zion said, "The LORD has forsaken me, And my Lord has forgotten me. Can a woman forget her nursing child, And not have compassion on the son of her womb? Surely they may forget, Yet I will not forget you. See, I have inscribed you on the palms of *My hands*..." (Isaiah 49:14-16 NKJV)

When we encounter the inevitable trials of life, may we remember the precedent set for us by Christ during this excruciating ordeal. We should measure all our suffering by the standard of His torment in order to bring proper perspective to our light, momentary trials. We do this knowing that they are yielding the same eternal glory as those trials that Christ suffered. The death of our own will gives life to the will of God that resides in all those who have accepted Christ Jesus.

For our light affliction, which is but for a moment, is working for us a far more exceeding *and* eternal weight of glory... (2 Corinthians 4:17 NKJV) For I consider that the sufferings of this present time are not worthy *to be compared* with the glory which shall be revealed in us. (Romans 8:18 NKJV)

A CLOSER LOOK

How many temptations have you successfully overcome in the last 18 hours?

Have you ever had a goal so worth pursuing that nothing could discourage you from reaching it? What was the primary encouragement that kept you on-course, and how can you apply it to your spiritual goals?

What personal comfort and assurance do you receive from knowing that your name is inscribed on the palms of Christ?

PETER'S DENIAL

But he denied it, saying, "I neither know nor understand what you are saying."
And he went out on the porch, and a rooster crowed. (Mark 14:68 NKJV)

Peter's denial wasn't just double talk from the man who always had something
straightforward to say. The original language indicates that Peter was making a
statement that went beyond denying just his allegiance to Christ. When he said
he did not know or understand, he was saying that, for him, Jesus did not even
exist. He was saying that not only was he not one of Jesus' disciples, but that he
had never even seen Jesus' face.

Although we may be quick to condemn Peter for his denial of Christ, we should not dismiss the roles that sovereignty and grace played in his denial. Peter, like us, was only able to know Christ to the extent that the Father revealed Him. The Bible says:

"All things have been delivered to Me by My Father, and no one knows the Son except the Father." (Matthew 11:27 NKJV) "No one can come to Me unless the Father who sent Me draws him..." (John 6:44 NKJV)

Jesus had forewarned Peter that he would deny Him. I had always thought it was for the benefit of proving to Peter that he could not rely on his flesh. This is, of course, an important lesson, as well, but as I now consider the destiny of this moment, there is another even more powerful and persuasive lesson: in the face of God's purposes and plans, nothing else will prevail. What God wants to accomplish will be accomplished regardless of what must take place to make it happen – even the denial of Christ on the part of a disciple whose heart was determined to never let it happen.

Many are the plans in a man's heart, but it is the Lord's purpose that prevails. (Proverbs 19:21 NIV)

In one instant – through one simple question from one insignificant servant girl – Peter went from being willing to die with Christ to vigorously denying Christ. Why? Even in his flesh, Peter should have been able to stand up to this little girl; but in the face of God's plan, Peter's determination faltered. God was establishing the importance of the reproof Christ had given to the disciples that apart from Him they could do nothing – not even recognize and acknowledge who He was! The apostle Paul makes the connection for us between God's glorious grace and its divine force to give us an understanding of Christ's sovereignty:

But when it pleased God, who separated me from my mother's womb and called *me* through His grace, to reveal His Son in me, that I might preach Him among the Gentiles, I did not immediately confer with flesh and blood... (Galatians 1:15-16 NKJV)

Paul understood that it was by the grace of God that Christ was revealed. It is in the withdrawal of this grace through God's sovereign plan that Peter stood completely alone and unable to identify the One for whom he had previously vowed to die.

Jesus forewarned Peter not for the sole purpose of learning the lesson that our flesh will fail, but for the purpose of letting us know that in the failure of our flesh, God is still in total and utter control.

A CLOSER LOOK

Can you recall a time when you were so afraid that your fear caused you to do something you thought you would never do?

Have you ever felt like you had completely failed only to find out that you were actually in the dead center of a spiritual lesson? Describe what you learned.

When you consider that God is sovereign, all-knowing, and all-powerful, what thoughts and feelings surface?

THE SILENCE THAT COMES WITH ASSURANCE

And the chief priests accused Him of many things, but He answered nothing. Then Pilate asked Him again, saying, "Do You answer nothing? See how many things they testify against You!" But Jesus still answered nothing, so that Pilate marveled. (Mark 15:3-5 NKJV)

What was so marvelous about Christ's silence? Why would it astound Pilate that Jesus did not feel compelled to give an answer to the multitude of accusations hurled against Him?

We have only to look at our own experience with accusation to understand Pilate's astonishment. It is human nature to defend oneself. When we are guilty, we defend our unacceptable actions with a long roster of rationalizations. When we are innocent, we refuse to give footing to the slightest finger-pointing; we declare our blamelessness to the bitter end. For Jesus to say nothing at all defied the very fiber of humanity, and this had Pilate puzzled.

In the heart of every one of us is the nagging need to always be right, even if we are wrong. This insatiable desire is linked to our longing to be loved. If we are found guilty of wrongdoing, we are then in jeopardy of being rejected. That fear forces into action the mechanisms of self-defense that will strive at all costs to keep us in a positive light. The fact that Christ seemed to be totally disconnected from this human quality caught Pilate's eye. It was magnified by the fact that Pilate was well aware of Christ's innocence. He had questioned Him extensively, and even been warned by his wife who had a dream confirming the Lord's blamelessness. Jesus' silence in the face of lying accusations spoke loudly to Pilate's heart concerning the personal, inner security that Christ demonstrated. Jesus did not have to defend Himself because He had complete trust in the Defender of His Soul, His Almighty Father.

...who, when He was reviled, did not revile in return; when He suffered, He did not threaten, but committed *Himself* to Him who judges righteously... (1 Peter 2:23 NKJV)

Pilate may not have fully connected the dots of Christ's disconnect from this human propensity to self-defend, but the calm assurance of Jesus' demeanor in the face of death definitely unnerved him.

It is a true test of our confidence in Christ when we are confronted by the accusations of the enemy. Can we withstand the temptation to defend ourselves with reasons for doing wrong or with our reputation for doing right?

I said, "I will guard my ways, Lest I sin with my tongue; I will restrain my mouth with a muzzle, While the wicked are before me." I was mute with silence, I held my peace *even* from good... (Psalm 39:1-2 NKJV)

Only if we are totally anchored in the assurance of our Father's love can we rest in a silent security of our acceptance, whether we are right or wrong. As we do so, a world bound by self-preservation and self-protection will marvel at the loud and clear message made by this silent act of surrender.

31

A CLOSER LOOK

When was the last time you were accused of something that you actually had done? How did you handle it?

Is it harder for you to remain silent when you are accused if you are wrong or if you are right? Explain.

How is the ability to not self-defend an exercise of your faith?

CARRYING THE CROSS

Then they compelled a certain man, Simon a Cyrenian, the father of Alexander and Rufus, as he was coming out of the country and passing by, to bear His cross. (Mark 15:21 NKJV)

It was a single instant, a seemingly indiscriminate decision that separated Simon from everyone else in the crowd. His call from God was encased in the harsh and brash command of the soldier, "Hey you! Get over here and pick up this cross and take it to the hill." Not what you would expect in the way of a divine appointment. Nonetheless, it was the turning point for this man from Africa. He had come to Jerusalem on unstated business; perhaps for the Passover, perhaps not. Regardless of what he came for, he found what he had been seeking his entire life.

The Bible states unequivocally that salvation and sanctification are of God. From the call to accept Christ until the call to come home, they are a work of God – start to finish:

"No one can come to Me unless the Father who sent Me draws him; and I will raise him up at the last day." (John 6:44 NKJV) Jesus said to him, "I am the way, the truth, and the life. No one comes to the Father except through Me." (John 14:6 NKJV)

God the Father had drawn Simon to this crossroad at that exact moment to meet Jesus. Their encounter would be the pivotal point in Simon's life. Simon's call was not unlike that of the unbeliever who goes systematically – and even mundanely – about his everyday life until the day he is confronted with an unavoidable situation. Whether it is a divorce, a death, a bankruptcy, or any myriad of other disappointments that come with this life, it is the moment of truth when God calls each one to pick up the cross of Christ.

Only in the unfailing mastery of the Holy Spirit's careful attention to detail do we discern the ripple effect of Simon's life-changing experience. Although nothing further is recorded of him, God makes a remote and often overlooked Scripture reference to Simon's family at the end of the book of Romans. As Paul closes this letter, he writes, "Greet Rufus, chosen in the Lord, and his mother and mine." (Romans 16:13 NKJV)

God gives us the names of Simon's children in Mark 15:21 so we can link the legacy of how this one providential encounter changed the course of his life. So dramatically and drastically did this event impact those in his household that they too were willing to pick up the cross and the cause of Christ. They were forever changed after having witnessed firsthand the way, the truth, and the life in Simon after he had carried the cross.

This biblical portrait of the cross' impact upon the life of one man speaks hope into our hearts about the influence that our own lives can have on those we love. If we, too, will be faithful to carry the cross of Christ, following Him to the hill of the crucifixion of our flesh, then others may become partakers of the invitation to salvation that Simon received on that God-appointed day of destiny in Jerusalem.

A CLOSER LOOK

What was the most unusual "divine appointment" you have ever experienced?

Can you remember a trial in your life that forced you to come face-to-face with God? What happened?

Who was or is the most influential person in your life concerning spiritual matters? Why?

WORTH THE PAIN

Likewise the chief priests also, mocking among themselves with the scribes, said, "He saved others; Himself He cannot save. Let the Christ, the King of Israel, descend now from the cross, that we may see and believe." Even those who were crucified with Him reviled Him. (Mark 15:31-32 NKJV)

Had it been you instead of Christ, at what point would you have broken and given way to the temptation to show these mocking fools a thing or two? Would it have been in the Garden of Gethsemane when they came to arrest you? How about when they had the dubious court hearings and brought in all the scoundrels they could find to lie about you? Or maybe when they brought you before Herod who made fun of you in front of his entire palace? Or when they had you blindfolded and beaten as they blasphemed and ridiculed you? Or would it have been when they drove the crown of thorns into your head, or before they drove the first of the nine-inch nails through your wrists and feet? At what point would you have said, "This is just not worth the pain"? Knowing that the power to do anything in the universe lies within a nanosecond of a thought, how long do you think you would have endured this kind of treatment?

Consider, too, the source of the insults. First, there were the scribes and elders who painstakingly transcribed every word of the book of Isaiah, but could not even recognize their Messiah as He hung plainly before them. Then there were soldiers who seemed to be amused at the misfortune of this 'misplaced' Messiah. There were the chief priests who should have been able to discern the deeds of God, if not the Word and face of God. And there were even the rogues of unrighteousness that hung on each side of the Righteous One. In their pathetic depths of depravity, they were dragged into the black hole of deception. Rather than realizing their helpless and hopeless condition, they reviled the innocent Man among them. How demeaning to be degraded by the dregs of society!

At what point would you have just had enough of this shallow charade of justice and trashed the whole idea of being Salvation incarnate? I don't know when it would have been too much for you, but I do know that I would have caved in long before it ever got so ugly or so violent. Yet Jesus did not, and that is what makes Him such an example of God's powerful grace and limitless mercy. Only God could have endured the temptation to save Himself instead of the whole world. This gives us the confidence that whatever we face, Jesus has been there and done that, and He is able to give us either the grace to overcome or the mercy to try again:

For we do not have a High Priest who cannot sympathize with our weaknesses, but was in all *points* tempted as *we are, yet* without sin. Let us therefore come boldly to the throne of grace, that we may obtain mercy and find grace to help in time of need. (Hebrews 4:15-16 NKJV)

The temptations of life will always be a struggle for our flesh, but this area of Scripture reminds us that we have a High Priest who has gone before us and who now lives in us so that we might have the victory over those temptations by the life of faith we now live in Him.

I have been crucified with Christ; it is no longer I who live, but Christ lives in me; and the life which I now live in the flesh I live by faith in the Son of God, who loved me and gave Himself for me. (Galatians 2:20 NKJV)

A CLOSER LOOK

What has been the hardest thing you have ever had to endure in your life?

How does knowing the cruelty and brutality that Jesus suffered on our behalf help you to endure your own suffering?

Why is it important to know that Jesus is our High Priest and that He is acquainted with every temptation known to man?

IN ONE BREATH

And Jesus cried out with a loud voice, and breathed His last. (Mark 15:37 NKJV)

Only through the eyes of faith can the remainder of this statement by Mark be understood. In the heavenly realm, it would read: "And Jesus cried out with a loud voice, and breathed His last **in this life**." The Bible teaches that when our temporal existence ends, our existence in eternity begins. We pass from one world into the next within the span of a single breath. There is no question that there is life after death; the only determination to be made is where it will be spent.

The master plan of the devil is to persuade us that the physical, touchable world in which we live and breathe is all there is to life. If he can convince us that we truly "only go around once in life, so get all the gusto we can get" or that we came from apes and will return to dust – or even return as a cow – then he has succeeded in his diabolical deception. But since the beginning, God has given us a physical witness of His unseen reality:

For since the creation of the world His invisible *attributes* are clearly seen, being understood by the things that are made, *even* His eternal power and Godhead, so that they are without excuse... (Romans 1:20 NKJV)

The Gospel of John states that Jesus is Light and offers light to all mankind:

That was the true Light which gives light to every man coming into the world. (John 1:9 NKJV)

Although we are bombarded daily with sights, sounds, smells, and sensations from this physical realm in which we exist, there is an outer and inner witness to the reality of God's existence. In our acknowledgement of that reality, we find the earthly death of this light-giving Savior to be of paramount importance. If we refuse to listen to the silent cry of creation and the inward longing of our hearts for the Creator, then we will only see a man hanging on the cross who breathed His last. But in the substance of things hoped for and in the evidence of things not seen – the true meaning of faith – we recognize a Righteous Messiah who breathed His last in this life so that, in one breath, we can stand face-to-face with Him when we transition from the unreal world of the physical realm to the real world of the Spirit.

As we embrace this truth, may we remember that we are only here, in this life, for a short season and that we must set our sights on heaven and give priority to the place in which we will live for all eternity.

Therefore we do not lose heart. Even though our outward man is perishing, yet the inward *man* is being renewed day by day. For our light affliction, which is but for a moment, is working for us a far more exceeding *and* eternal weight of glory, while we do not look at the things which are seen, but at the things which are not seen. For the things which are seen *are* temporary, but the things which are not seen *are* eternal. (2 Corinthians 4:16-18 NKJV)

A CLOSER LOOK

What are some of the inner and outer witnesses in your life of the reality of God's existence?

Why is faith so important in dealing with death?

What are some ways to exercise faith in the midst of all the sights, sounds, smells, and sensations of the physical realm?

THE IMMOVABLE STONE

Very early in the morning, on the first *day* of the week, they came to the tomb when the sun had risen. And they said among themselves, "Who will roll away the stone from the door of the tomb for us?" (Mark 16:2-3 NKJV)

Odd that the obstacle that Mary Magdalene, Mary, the mother of James, and Salome thought would keep them from being able to see their beloved Messiah was the object that their forefathers had used to memorialize God's revelations. Every time God had made an impact upon the nation of Israel, or on the heart of one of its leaders, an altar was built from stones so the event could be remembered forever. These stones of remembrance dotted the pathway of God's children from Egypt to the Promised Land, marking out every act of mercy and miraculous provision of grace that testified of the holy Hand of their heavenly Father.

Not unlike the stones of old, the large, immovable stone that these women expected to find at the mouth of the tomb was yet another monument of remembrance. This stone was God's memorial of His ultimate act of mercy and final provision of grace. This stone testified to God's journey with man from the bondage of sin in the Garden of Eden to the entry of humankind into the eternal Promised Land of freedom in Christ. God had walked every step of the way with His people.

But when they looked up, they saw that the stone, which was very large, had been rolled away. (Mark 16:4 NIV)

The stone that no human could have rolled away had been removed and set aside as a memorial. Just as sin had set in place a heart of stone as a memorial, keeping out the grace by which man could be saved, now God, through the sacrifice of His Only Son, had removed it. What man had been unable to do, God did for him in the death of His Son. For all those who looked at the stone removed from the mouth of the tomb, there would be a testament of the finished work of Christ, once and for all bringing unity between God and His children.

"Then I will give them one heart, and I will put a new spirit within them, and take the stony heart out of their flesh, and give them a heart of flesh, that they may walk in My statutes and keep My judgments and do them; and they shall be My people, and I will be their God." (Ezekiel 11:19-20 NKJV)

Likewise for us, the immovable stone rolled away from the empty tomb is also our stone of remembrance to remind us that what we were unable to do for ourselves, God did for us through His Son. As we come to God through Christ's sacrifice, we find the unity and fellowship with Him for which we were created. We then become living stones for others to look upon and see the reality of the Risen Savior living in us:

Coming to Him *as to* a living stone, rejected indeed by men, but chosen by God *and* precious, you also, as living stones, are being built up a spiritual house, a holy priesthood, to offer up spiritual sacrifices acceptable to God through Jesus Christ. (1 Peter 2:4-5 NKJV)

A CLOSER LOOK

In what ways do you memorialize important events in your life?

What stones in your life has God removed?

How have the 'immovable stone' events of your life brought God into others' awareness?

THE OPEN GRAVE

And entering the tomb, they saw a young man clothed in a long white robe sitting on the right side; and they were alarmed. (Mark 16:5 NKJV)

The courage of these women at the open grave is astounding. The stone that could only be moved by the efforts of many men had been rolled away. Who, besides them, would have even wanted to go into the tomb? It had to have crossed their minds that whoever moved the stone might still be there. They had to have known that their lives could be in danger, yet they entered the open grave, as if compelled by an unstoppable force. And much to their surprise and alarm, they found a young man, clothed in a long white robe, sitting to the right of where Jesus had been laid.

At this point, curiosity causes us to question why God had this heavenly messenger sitting on the inside of the tomb. Why would He not have placed him outside the tomb? What if the women had panicked at seeing that the stone was moved and just run away? God could certainly have had the young man show up along the road to the tomb and encourage the women, but instead He placed him strategically inside the open grave. Why? Because the Bible tells us that only by those who come searching for Him with all their heart can He be found:

And you will seek Me and find *Me*, when you search for Me with all your heart. (Jeremiah 29:13 NKJV)

God placed the answer to the barrage of questions that must have been pummeling these women's minds inside the tomb – not on the outside, not on the way, but in the very heart of the tomb of Christ. They had to be willing to risk their lives to find their answer – the Messiah of God.

Two thousand years later, nothing has changed. Those who desire to find the Messiah, to follow Christ, must come holding nothing back. They must be willing to search for Him with whole hearts, even to the point of entering the tomb of His death.

"He who finds his life will lose it, and he who loses his life for My sake will find it." (Matthew 10:39 NKJV)

Do we have the same relentless determination for Christ that these women had? In the face of impossible odds, are we willing to go anywhere to find Him? As we struggle with sins like pride, self-sufficiency, anger, and a harsh tongue, do we possess the faith and courage to still make our way to the place where Christ paid the price for them? If we are willing to enter the grave of death-to-self, we can rest assured that we, too, will find the glorious message of the resurrection – that God has rolled away every stone of sin and, through Christ's death, brought us new life in Him:

Therefore we were buried with Him through baptism into death, that just as Christ was raised from the dead by the glory of the Father, even so we also should walk in newness of life. For if we have been united together in the likeness of His death, certainly we also shall be *in the likeness of His* resurrection, knowing this, that our old man was crucified with *Him*, that the body of sin might be done away with, that we should no longer be slaves of sin. For he who has died has been freed from sin. (Romans 6:4-7 NKJV)

A CLOSER LOOK

Have you ever been driven forward despite your fear? What were the circumstances and your motivation?

If the women's determination to find Christ was 100 on a scale of 1 to 100, where would your own determination be? Explain why.

What are some of the stones of sin that keep you from turning to Christ?

How does knowing that Jesus died to remove every obstacle that stands between you and Him change your attitude about approaching Him?

THE EMPTY TOMB

The resurrection: Jesus Christ, God in the flesh, living a sinless life, dying on a cross for the sins of the world, and then rising from the dead.

Christians (and even some non-Christians) have no problem accepting this tenet of the faith. This same group of agreeing people diminishes dramatically, however, when it comes to the resurrection of the dead in Christ and the living at His return – an event described in the Bible and coined by Bible scholars as the Rapture.

...And the dead in Christ will rise first. Then we who are alive and remain shall be caught up together with them in the clouds to meet the Lord in the air. And thus we shall always be with the Lord. (1 Thessalonians 4:16b-17 NKJV)

Christ's resurrection was a foreshadowing of our resurrection – so why the disbelief? The Rapture holds the same stigma in our day as the Flood did in Noah's day. God had told Noah to build a boat because He was going to flood the earth. Not so hard to grasp, unless, of course, you take into consideration that in Noah's day there had never been any rain. As crazy as Noah seemed to his contemporaries, so the modern-day believer seems to his generation when he casually mentions the Rapture. This is understandable when you realize that both events require faith in order to be understood. At the time that each was first proclaimed, neither had been witnessed, considered, or even imagined before – but as sure as the Great Flood became a fact even to the scientific world – so shall the Rapture become a fact to those who are left behind.

The empty tomb foreshadows the empty homes, the empty beds, the empty cars, the empty stores, the empty schools, and the empty hearts that will remain after God removes His people from the earth. Don't be one of those who say, "Oh, that will never happen. That's just another end-of-the-world story that every generation for centuries has been telling!" Heed the apostle Peter's warning:

...knowing this first: that scoffers will come in the last days, walking according to their own lusts, and saying, "Where is the promise of His coming? For since the fathers fell asleep, all things continue as *they were* from the beginning of creation." For this they willfully forget: that by the word of God the heavens were of old, and the earth standing out of water and in the water, by which the world *that* then existed perished, being flooded with water. But the heavens and the earth *which* are now preserved by the same word, are reserved for fire until the day of judgment and perdition of ungodly men. But, beloved, do not forget this one thing, that with the Lord one day *is* as a thousand years, and a thousand years as one day. The Lord is not slack concerning *His* promise, as some count slackness, but is longsuffering toward us, not willing that any should perish but that all should come to repentance. (2 Peter 3:3-9 NKJV)

To those who did not respond to the empty tomb, God gives one last opportunity to believe. It is my prayer that everyone who reads these words will respond to God's invitation to eternal life through Jesus Christ. Don't wait for the Rapture to believe. Let Christ's already-empty tomb be the reality that convinces you that God is able to do what He has promised. Don't be like those of Noah's day who literally drowned in their disbelief. Don't be left behind because you believe that this shocking, massive, catastrophic event is impossible.

But Jesus looked at them and said, "With men *it is* impossible, but not with God; for with God all things are possible." (Mark 10:27 NKJV)

A CLOSER LOOK

Do you find it hard to believe in something that has never happened before? Why or why not?

What is your understanding of the Rapture of the Church?

Think about and then write a description of how you think it would feel to wake up the morning after the Rapture and realize that all the Christians are gone.

Why would it be comforting to know that Jesus is coming back for those who love Him?

THE INTIMACY OF
THE RESURRECTED CHRIST

Now when *He* rose early on the first *day* of the week, He appeared first to Mary Magdalene, out of whom He had cast seven demons. She went and told those who had been with Him, as they mourned and wept. (Mark 16:9-10 NKJV)

How apropos that Jesus' exit was as mind-boggling as His entrance. Rather than the prophecy-fulfilling birth of the Messiah taking place in a royal palace surrounded by the fanfare of kings and nations, it happened in a filthy barn amidst the donkeys and cattle, witnessed only by a young peasant girl and a lowly carpenter.

Rather than the fulfillment of the ancient prophecy of resurrection being displayed to the entire palace guard, Pilate, or even the chief religious leaders, Christ appeared instead to Mary Magdalene, a rehabilitated prostitute who had formerly been demon-possessed.

These events truly magnify how utterly unimpressed God is with our man-made hierarchies and value systems. Where we might consider His decisions wasted opportunities to stun the world, He is not remotely moved by our ideas of how and what He should do to impact the world with the gospel message. He is only interested in the cry of a heart that longs to love Him in an intimate act of abandonment. Mary Magdalene did not hold a position of prestige that would have qualified her to be the recipient of the most important moment in human history and all eternity; she simply had a heart that loved Christ more than anything else in this world.

Jesus had rightly revealed the heart of God in His response to Simon, who considered the woman that anointed Jesus' feet with her tears so unworthy that she shouldn't have even been in the same house with the Lord:

"Therefore I say to you, her sins, *which are* many, are forgiven, for she loved much. But to whom little is forgiven, *the same* loves little." (Luke 7:47 NKJV)

God's priority is not grandiose demonstrations of His divine magic. His priority is showing Himself intimately to those who are broken and contrite. As Christ stated emphatically:

"But go and learn what this means: *'I desire mercy and not sacrifice.'* For I did not come to call the righteous, but sinners, to repentance." (Matthew 9:13 NKJV)

It is no wonder that God does not waste His displays of miracles and mercy upon those who have no heart for them. If we do not understand our own sinful condition, then the value of His precious gift is lost in the legalism of our own self-righteousness. Only in the Light that reveals our need for forgiveness can we comprehend the proposal of love that was made at the cross. It is an offer that will not be apparent to everyone – only to those who have the humility to recognize the royalty of the Resurrected One amidst the mundane peasantry of humanity.

If we long to have Jesus reveal Himself to us, we must put away all pretenses of self-righteousness and realize our need for His forgiveness. Then we can find the appreciation that fuels the fire of a thankful heart and draws the attention of a perfect Savior. He is risen and appears intimately to those who love Him outlandishly.

A CLOSER LOOK

When you consider that God is not impressed with our outward accomplishments, but only with our inward character, what happens in your heart and mind?

Are you prone to self-righteousness? How does that hinder your relationship and communication with God?

Have you ever experienced a miracle or a move of God? What was your heart's condition at the time?

REALIZING THE RESURRECTION

Later He appeared to the eleven as they sat at the table; and He rebuked their unbelief and hardness of heart, because they did not believe those who had seen Him after He had risen. (Mark 16:14 NKJV)

What an incredible picture of the profound importance of God's Word. The eleven apostles had heard it from the women, they had heard it from the two disciples who met Jesus on the road to Emmaus, but now the Living Word appeared to them personally – and with a rebuke.

The Bible tells us that all Scripture is God-breathed and good for doctrine, reproof, correction, and instruction in righteousness. So, is it any wonder that in Luke's account of this same rebuke, Christ reminded His disciples what was written in Old Testament Scripture?

Then He said to them, "These *are* the words which I spoke to you while I was still with you, that all things must be fulfilled which were written in the Law of Moses and the Prophets and *the* Psalms concerning Me." And He opened their understanding, that they might comprehend the Scriptures. (Luke 24:44-45 NKJV)

Christ's rebuke was not that the apostles had failed to believe the testimony of the women or the other witnesses, but that they had failed to believe His previous Word to them, which He had given from the Law of Moses and Books of the Prophets and the Psalms. After He delivered this word of rebuke, He then did what only God is able to do – He opened their understanding to grasp what He had just said.

With all the time that Jesus had spent personally instructing His disciples, and with the personal testimony of eyewitnesses to His resurrection, these men still were only able to believe the Good News by the power of the Holy Spirit. He alone is able to help the human mind and heart conceive and understand spiritual things.

"Nevertheless I tell you the truth. It is to your advantage that I go away; for if I do not go away, the Helper will not come to you; but if I depart, I will send Him to you." (John 16:7 NKJV)

For what man knows the things of a man except the spirit of the man which is in him? Even so no one knows the things of God except the Spirit of God…But the natural man does not receive the things of the Spirit of God, for they are foolishness to him; nor can he know *them*, because they are spiritually discerned. (1 Corinthians 2:11, 14 NKJV)

Although we wish we could have walked and talked with Jesus face-to-face, according to these Scriptures, we have an even greater capacity to know God and the truth of His Word by the power of God's Spirit dwelling in us. By yielding our minds and hearts to Him, He is able to make us understand His Word so that we may know the reality of the Risen Savior for ourselves.

A CLOSER LOOK

Have you ever had a problem understanding God's Word? If so, take a minute and pray that the Holy Spirit would illuminate it for you.

If you had lived during the time of Jesus' earthly ministry, write down what questions you would have asked Him.

Using a concordance, look up keywords from each of your questions and see what His Word says about that area of your life.

COMMISSION BIRTHED FROM CONVICTION

And He said to them, "Go into all the world and preach the gospel to every creature." (Mark 16:15 NKJV)

Talk about faith. Consider the group Jesus was talking to at that very moment – a bunch of cowardly men that were burdened with unbelief and hard hearts. They weren't even able to stand with Christ when He was going through His most difficult moment in all of ministry. Yet, with the far-reaching sight of God, He commissioned them to take the gospel into the entire world.

As ironic, and even ludicrous, as this scene may seem, it is the backdrop for the most necessary ingredient in the fulfillment of the Great Commission. Jesus knew these eleven men were not even capable of seeing a vision of this magnitude, but He also knew that it would not be them who accomplished the mission. It would be the Holy Spirit moving through the disciples that would eventually fulfill the Master's command.

A commission birthed from conviction – it is the quintessential picture of the corrective hand of God. Rebuke followed by direction – this is the pattern of the Holy Spirit's work in the believer's life:

"And when He has come, He will convict the world of sin, and of righteousness, and of judgment..." (John 16:8 NKJV)

Once Jesus had chided the disciples for their lack of faith, He then imparted to them the direction that would put them on a path of belief so strong that it would overcome every obstacle, even unto their own deaths.

When we fail, we can be sure that Satan will be nearby to condemn us. But Jesus is even closer to convict us. How will we tell the difference? The answer is in this pattern: Satan simply condemns and leaves us feeling worthless; the Spirit's conviction will never come without direction. The Spirit corrects us, instructs us, and leaves us with a hope, a future, and a purpose.

We must remember that we can do nothing – great or small – apart from God's Spirit. By the power of God's Spirit, on the other hand, nothing is impossible. Therefore, when we fail, our failure may be an indicator that we have somehow stepped out of the leading of the indwelling Christ. Instead of giving in through guilt and discouragement to the condemnation and accusations of the enemy, we can listen for that still, small voice that will give us correction and instruction. Then, as we slip out of our inadequacy into His sufficiency, we will be ready to preach the gospel throughout our own little worlds:

So we have been sent to speak for Christ. It is as if God is calling to you through us. We speak for Christ when we beg you to be at peace with God. (2 Corinthians 5:20 ICB)

A CLOSER LOOK

Have you ever felt inadequate in sharing your faith with someone else? How does the condition of the disciples when they were commissioned help bolster your courage?

How can you discern between what is condemnation and what is conviction?

Reflect on a time when your failure was an indicator that you had stepped out of the leading of the Spirit. What did you learn?

ROYAL REUNION

So then, after the Lord had spoken to them, He was received up into heaven, and sat down at the right hand of God. (Mark 16:19 NKJV)

Can you imagine how this royal reunion must have felt? It would be hard to envision the magnitude of emotion that overwhelmed – not just Jesus – but the entire Host of heaven and the passionate heart of God as Christ left the earth and entered the throne room to sit next to His Father. The heavenly realm had watched Him intensely from the time of His birth. They had observed His every encounter: the miracles, the debates with the Pharisees, and His power over death at the tomb of Lazarus. They had held their breath in the wilderness, wondering if this second Adam would fall to the temptations of the sly, shining one like the first Adam had. They observed every tender moment He spent with His disciples and how He had turned the hearts of sinners back to God through His mercy, patience, and lovingkindness. They had watched in horror His cruel and shocking death on the cross. They had been there that first Easter morning to experience the glory of the resurrection. And now, after what had seemed like an eternity, all of heaven stood watching as Jesus crossed the finish line of His race.

The scene had to have put any Hollywood production to shame. The Hero of all heroes, the original Good Guy was finally taking His rightful place at the right hand of God Almighty. As unbelievably joyful as this occasion must have been, today the Son of God awaits what will be for Him an even more glorious occasion – the day that you and I step through that portal of heaven, the day that the fruit of His righteous mission comes to fruition, the day that He is able to receive us into the heavenly Kingdom with the words that we long to hear:

"Well *done*, good and faithful servant; you have been faithful over a few things, I will make you ruler over many things. Enter into the joy of your lord." (Matthew 25:23 NKJV)

This joy was what Jesus saw as He hung on the cross. In the tortured and tormented hours of His crucifixion, He was given a vision by God of the day we would be able to enter heaven because of His sacrifice that opened the door of saving faith for all who would follow:

Let us look only to Jesus. He is the one who began our faith, and he makes our faith perfect. Jesus suffered death on the cross. But he accepted the shame of the cross as if it were nothing. He did this because of the joy that God put before him. And now he is sitting at the right side of God's throne. (Hebrews 12:2 ICB)

The key to our faith is fixing our eyes on Jesus. He is the One who procured our salvation and ignited our faith, and He is the One who holds us securely in His love until we reach the fullness of our faith. It will be His joy at that time to receive us and to beckon for us to take our seat with Him.

But God, who is rich in mercy, because of His great love with which He loved us... made us alive together with Christ... and raised *us* up together, and made *us* sit together in the heavenly *places* in Christ Jesus... (Ephesians 2:4-6 NKJV)

A CLOSER LOOK

Have you ever experienced a homecoming – either yours or someone else's? What was it like?

Think about a time when you completed a long project. What feelings did you experience?

Picture the most elaborate wedding banquet you can. Now, meditate upon our heavenly banquet and seeing Jesus' face when we enter heaven. What will be your first words to Him?

What would have made it worth the pain that Christ suffered? Why would He have endured the endless hours of mockery, the rejection of humanity, and the separation from Divinity? What was in it for Him? Through these devotionals, you will get a glimpse into the end of Christ's life on earth – the Last Supper, the betrayal, the denial, the agony of the cross, the glory of the resurrection, and His royal reunion in heaven with the Father. As you walk the path with Him, don't be surprised when you find that the startling answer to the question of what made it worth it to Him - is you.

For He made Him who knew no sin to be sin for us,
that we might become the righteousness of God in Him.

2 CORINTHIANS 5:21 NKJV

ISBN 1-932283-08-0

9 781932 283082